Reflections from silence

Richard D. Hathaway is Professor Emeritus of English, State University of New York at New Paltz. A member of the Religious Society of Friends since 1951, he was deeply involved in the peace movement in the 1950's '60's, and '70's and in the civil-rights movement in the 1960's.

Helen Rowlands is head of education at Woodbrooke Quaker study centre, UK.

Reflections from silence

Richard D. Hathaway

for Viola's guardian angel, Judy Pike
Dick Hathaway

QUAKERbooks

First published July 2011

Quaker Books, Friends House, 173 Euston Road, London NW1 2BJ

www.quaker.org.uk

ISBN 978-1-907123-20-7

Book design and typesetting Golden Cockerel Press Ltd, London
Cover design by Quaker Communications

Front cover photo by John Angerson

Printed by RAP spiderweb, Manchester

Acknowledgements:

Extract from 'There was a Saviour', from *The Poems* by Dylan Thomas (Orion Books), used with kind permission.

Extract from *The colour purple* by Alice Walker (Orion Books), used with kind permission.

Extract from Theodore Roethke, Selected Poems, ed. Edward Hirsch used with kind permission of Faber and Faber Ltd.

INTRODUCTION

It is an unusual thing for a Friend to write down the spoken ministry they have given in meeting for worship, and even more unusual for that practice to be carried out for many years. To what end might they do it? Might it be a feeling that one's words spoken in meeting have particular weight and should be remembered? Might the otherwise transitory words come to form a sort of spiritual journal, a record of the journey of one particular soul, of one individual's faithful strivings to follow where they are led in worship? Could they in fact become helpful to others, showing a little of what spoken ministry can be like, and continuing to have meaning, even beyond the contexts in which the messages were originally given? It is with this latter hope that they are being published now.

The ministry recorded here was given by a North American Friend, Richard Hathaway, who is a member of New York Yearly Meeting. Friends in that yearly meeting have a range of religious backgrounds and theological persuasions, including those who do and those who do not identify themselves as Christian. Some of its worship is based in silence and is very similar to that experienced in most British and European meetings; other meetings hold more programmed worship and appoint Friends to serve as pastors. Poughkeepsie Meeting, Richard Hathaway's home meeting, which is mentioned in the text, worships in the unprogrammed tradition. The yearly meeting is one of those which is affiliated to two of the North American umbrella organisations, Friends General Conference and Friends United Meeting, and thus seeks to live creatively with the tension of recognising that there is no single, simple way of giving voice to spiritual experience.

In an unprogrammed meeting for worship, Quakers seek to still themselves in the presence of one another and to open themselves to the workings of the spirit at the heart of life. Out of the silence, ministry may flow. Sometimes ministry may be given in song or in spoken prayer, but most usually in our times Friends reflect upon experience, seeking meaning in their lives, in the lives of others and in events in the world. Often a message will be augmented by reference to scriptures, to literature or to some other universalising or deepening point of reference. In this book, we have chosen to leave such references unmarked, since they may also have been either familiar or unfamiliar to those who heard them when the ministry was first spoken.

If stilling ourselves towards deep inner silence is the aim of Quaker worship, why not always remain entirely in silence, as is the case in some religious practices (and indeed the case in some particular meetings for worship)? George Fox, writing in 1657, put it like this:

> Concerning silent meeting: the intent of all speaking is to bring
> in to the life, and to walk in and to possess the same, and to
> live in and enjoy it and to feel Gods presence, and that is in the
> silence (not in the wandering, whirling, tempestuous part of
> man or woman); for there is the flock lying down at the noon-
> day, and feeding of the bread of life, and drinking at the springs
> of life, when they do not speak words; for words declared are to
> bring people to it, and confessing God's goodness and love as
> they are moved by the eternal God and his spirit.

So he is saying that we can feel God's presence in the silence, indeed we need the silence to still our tempestuous natures, but spoken ministry can help deepen our understanding; help us dwell in that place; help us walk more faithfully through our lives. A test we might apply to ministry is: does it help us move into the Light; does it help us know God; does it help us live well? Perhaps, as you read the pieces of ministry which follow, you will find some have these qualities for you.

Reflecting on such questions might tend to make us think that every piece of ministry should be deep and profound. This record shows us that it is not always so. Sometimes a piece of ministry gives oblique glimpses of the spirit: it is almost as if the spirit is speaking from a hidden place and we only see its faint shadow. Perhaps its importance for us then lies as much in the faithfulness of our own attempts at meaning-making as we listen as it does in the content of the message.

If you choose to read these 'reflections' straight through at one sitting, you will get a sense of the sweep of one Friend's spoken ministry, a privileged glimpse into the movements of spirit in an individual's life. Some themes, some preoccupations, emerge: the nature of light and the need to go through darkness to come into light; the nature of God and how we can know anything of God; the need to take risks in the spiritual life, to dare to do what is uncomfortable; the nature of 'home' and the true meaning of Christmas and Easter.

You will also see how the giving of spoken ministry may ebb and flow in a person's life – times when messages come close together, with hints of the stimulus of a lively yearly meeting gathering or of the struggles of a committee seeking unity in decision-making; other times when years pass with no messages recorded. You will see how ministry can 'take over' the speaker, and the message can change even in the giving of it. What is not recorded here are the discernment processes which led to giving a particular piece of ministry – was it well discerned, rightly led? Only those who were present at the time can be judges of that. Yet we can still ask ourselves the question, does this ministry speak to me, now? For this, a slower, more reflective reading may help. You may wish to take one piece at a time and ask yourself:

- What in this message rings true for me?
- What in my own life does it touch?
- How does this message help me feel God's presence and walk more faithfully in the light?

Advices & queries 12 gives practical advice about listening to other people's ministry in meeting for worship:

> Receive the vocal ministry of others in a tender and creative spirit. Reach for the meaning deep within it, recognising that even if it is not God's word for you, it may be so for others.

You may want to apply this to your reading too: to read a passage, taste and either savour for a while or respectfully let it go. Remember it was first offered as ministry, and is still offered as ministry here.

Helen Rowlands 8.10.10

I offer these Quaker tidbits raw, unrevised, just as they were spoken in meetings for worship, then written down a few hours later. Only once in my life have I given a prepared message in an unprogrammed meeting. It was in January 1967, when I was visiting Scarsdale Meeting to recruit supporters for the Easter Pilgrimage to the Peace Bridge, a nonviolent direct-action project for sending medical supplies to both South Vietnam and North Vietnam in violation of US administrative policy. That message is not among those recorded below.

I think that God is a very big elephant and that I am a blind man. Or sometimes I think God is a kangaroo, because when I reach out to touch him, he's jumped to somewhere else. Sometimes the very name 'God' seems too glib and brings to mind something too small for whatever it is that's out there that I touch and can't see, and I think that we should consider changing names. I think the word 'Light' would be a way of saying it better, except that that's too small too. I think that what is out there and in here is more than just light. God includes the darkness too. When we start thinking about God and when we put on our meeting faces, I think we close off a great deal of our minds. We need to open ourselves to all that is.

When we speak of God we start speaking biblical language and concepts or Query-and-Discipline language, and when we come to meeting we think and talk too exclusively about behaviour and action. We are too human-centred, too moralistic in our religious concern. We need more than just the inner light in man. God does more than just tell us what to do.

If we are first blinded, we will receive new eyes. We need to see the outer light too. To see the outer light we need to become blind. We can't see the outer light if we are seeing instead the temptations, the clamour, the dazzle of the everyday, materialistic world of the television, the street, the laundry. To see the outer light is to see the mass of sunlight that moves in shifting images. It is to see what Sophocles saw: the tragic weight and pull and dazzle of this wrenching, terrible, glorious world that tears a person open. It is when we are broken open and blinded to the world of ordinary reality that we become able to see the outer light. The outer light is in this crimson and gold wonder that flares at me from every side in this autumn season. And I do not mean just the leaves, beautiful as they are. That's too external. I am thinking of the veins of gold running in the rocks. The very rocks are melted under the pressure of eternity.

[3 November 1968]

* * *

Living on the edge is difficult and dangerous. You might fall off. There might not be anybody out there to catch you. It was easy after Columbus had shown the way, pushing back the devils of doubt. Men and sheep tend to huddle together in flocks. It's warm there. It's very seldom that one of them goes counter to the main direction or wanders very far from the centre. It's hard to be daring, when you can't be sure that you're right. When our morality is based upon experience, it tells us little besides what has proved expedient in a given situation. Our morality is a computerised calculus of expediencies, an account book, a ledger, a log, telling us where we've been. And so we fold up and fail.

[1 March 1970]

* * *

I want to say a good word for Scrooge, who was a Quaker and foresaw where all that Christmas goose was leading us – to the Ford-ising of holiday goodwill. Dylan Thomas speaks of "silk-and-rough love." Ralph Waldo Emerson said "Your goodness must have some edge to it". And it was Emerson who amazingly stated, contradicting the whole direction of his usual optimism, "The doctrine of hatred must be preached as the counteraction of the

doctrine of love when that pules and whines." And Melville, in
one of his great dark moments, said that "however baby man may
brag of his science and skill... yet for ever and for ever, to the crack
of doom, the sea will insult and murder him, and pulverize the
stateliest, stiffest frigate he can make". And Camus's Meursault, at
the end, as he awaits an unjust death by execution, contemplates
the "benign indifference of the universe" with a kind of calm
ecstasy, and we feel the grandeur of a universe that is hard and
grey and cold. We must feel the ocean of dark to feel the ocean of
light, that flows over it. The festival of lights comes at the darkest
time of the year.

[20 December 1970]

* * *

Someone said to me "Where is this inner light people talk about?"
I answered that if a person was having a hard time locating his inner
light it was probably because he was sitting on it. To see the inner
light thee has to lift up thy self and walk.

[April 1971]

* * *

I live in the shadow of six or seven gigantic trees: an elm and several
willows, with large, spreading, arching branches. First the elm
dropped its leaves and now finally the willows. Then, just when
to most people the world is reaching its grey, Novembery phase,
suddenly inside the sun comes in.

[19 November 1972]

* * *

I am learning negative capability: how to remain in a condition
of optimism and faith when all the particular providences and
evidences which had served as bases for my faith have been cut from
under me. Once having achieved a state of faith, based on particular
evidences, the state of faith is its own validation, needing no props,

day to day, outside itself. This is the state to which I am being disciplined by having my props removed.

[Winter/spring 1974]

* * *

We are surrounded by a great cloud of witnesses. It's like the Milky Way, spangling the night. If you close your eyes you can see it, like the Magellanic Clouds in intergalactic space.

Yesterday I saw a huge, perfect rose – a real, literal rose – all covered with dozens of drops of dew, each a perfect pearl. I was reminded of Dante's vision of the saints in heaven in concentric rings of light, streaming like rose petals from the central point of God's radiance. I thought of the photograph I have of a drop of dew on the end of a leaf of grass, greatly magnified. The dewdrop is a perfect orb, a lens, and through it the sky and the landscape are projected, inverted.

The cloud of witnesses is everywhere, and it's also in specific places. This morning I saw 62 of them gathered. There were tears in many of their eyes and smiles of joy on their faces. Their love is reaching out to us here. God's love and peace are reaching out to us. It's a free gift. Accept it.

[30 June 1974; reference is to the morning sing at Tres Dias]

* * *

Lord, I forgot to prepare a place for you.
There was only straw and a musty manger.
But it didn't matter.
You came anyway.

[Christmas 1976]

* * *

The words of yesterday are dead. Tomorrow's words are not yet known to me.

I am like a hen, delivering my one egg a day and then cackling and clucking.

We are like sponges: we can know only as much of God as our thirst prepares us to hold.

[23 October 1977]

* * *

I have never been able to store up God for future use. I am only able to experience as much of God as I am able to actually use, only so much as I need to enable me to take risks, to grow, to love, to build something with. What I need is there when it is required. It is like the spider that I see swinging across to attach his strand. As he swings, the silk flows out of his own gut, just enough to keep the tension right for his swing. When he hits the far side the flow stops and he attaches the silk as it instantly solidifies. Then he goes on to the next strand until the web is finished. There is always the ideal pattern to guide him instinctively as the web flows and then solidifies, and there is always the difference as the web is adapted to the shape of the space it occupies. When it is finished the sun comes to its shining. And then the web is torn down to be built again.

[23 July 1978]

* * *

I don't feel as much pressure inside me to speak in meeting as I used to. I'd like to think this is because of increasing wisdom, but I'm afraid it's caused by mental sluggishness or, more likely, spiritual sloth. I'm sure that all of us here remember times when we felt close to the root of things, had experiences of deep spiritual gathering. There were times when I felt this whole yearly meeting on the move and doing things and felt God's presence leading us. We took risks, and there was a sense of adventure. Now, I confess, on a sleepy Sunday afternoon, perhaps at Quarterly Meeting, I feel a bit drony and wheezy. Where have all the flowers gone? What I want to say is that there's a danger of using the draining away of spiritual energies as an excuse. Because we don't have the spiritual zing at the moment, we can just sit back and say, well I don't have it anymore. We can even begin to feel satisfied with this state of affairs. After all, real religion is a lot of trouble. And we can say that because we aren't doing anything big, or dramatic, or prophetic we can't really be close to God. Pretty soon God's presence gets rather blurry, unreal. We are beating ourselves over the head with our sense of unworthiness and using that as an excuse for not having a spiritual life. Guilt, whether profound and dramatic, or of the commonplace garden variety, can stop up the whole spiritual drainage and renewal system. Jonathan Edwards's uncle, Joseph Hawley, committed suicide in a fit of religious despair, presumably because the contrast between the spiritual magnificence he remembered and the drabness of his present condition made him feel excluded from the Kingdom. So that's why Rachel's words came home to me, about how the Lord spoke to her anyway. As the saying goes, Praise the Lord anyway.

[9 June 1985]

* * *

[At Yearly Meeting, someone tried to speak into a microphone that wasn't plugged in.]

I think we have just seen a parable enacted: You have to be plugged in to a source of power, *the* source of power, before you can be connected to other people.

[3 August 1985]

* * *

People who aren't satisfied with a this-worldly parousia, who want something better than grace in this present life, want time to stop. They want God to come and stop time and take over. Or they want a heavenly dictator who will see to it that everything is perfect. But 'perfect' in Greek means finished, which means dead, not having the possibility of growth. God didn't buy that idea. He started the idea of time and growth and decay and death, which means imperfection. Those who are demanding perfection are impatient people, and the world they are asking for is dead, like a painting that is finished. That is all very well for art galleries, but God's idea is not to fill up the art galleries but to have a lot of painters and painting studios in which creation is constantly going on. The painter has the best of the painting. Of course, this analogy is not exact, because even the act of appreciating a work of art is a creative act, and we mustn't think of paintings as dead. They do have an ongoing life. But the life in them is not in the paint: it is in the eye of the beholder.

[4 August 1985]

* * *

Just as the Hebrews in the Exodus found that there was manna for one day and that they could not store it up because it got worms in it after one day, we discover that we get just enough light to see our next step down the road. Some people want all the answers at once: they don't want to take truth day by day. When I was in college I had a philosophy course and the professor told us that the German idealist Hegel had constructed a perfect system in which all the parts were logically connected and proven. The only trouble was that the system couldn't be proven to have any connection with the real world. So I decided that I didn't need to spend any time reading Hegel, because the only kind of truth I was interested in was what applied to the real world.

I have noticed that some people are attracted to leaders that have all the answers and are very confident they have the truth. They want something or someone to follow that gives them security of finality. They are attracted therefore to things that are perfect and finished. But that's the trouble. What is perfect and finished is also dead and doesn't have the potentiality for growth. Friends, I think, are more attracted to those who aren't so sure that they have final truth. I noticed at Yearly Meeting that they tended to shy away from those who were sure that the final answers to things could be found in the words of Jesus or the words of George Fox. It wasn't that there was any lack of truth in the words of Jesus or Fox. It was a distrust of the idea that you could grab hold of an abstraction and then stop thinking. It was a distrust of words that hadn't been earned by experience and that were someone else's words, of words that didn't seem to apply to their present experience. The words that meet their present needs are harder to come by.

[4 August 1985]

* * *

Without darkness the light of the candle would not be visible.
Without silence, we could not hear people's voices.
Without absence, we would not be conscious of presence.
Help me to light my candle, Lord.

[1 December 1985]

* * *

Trying for the moment to think like a sociologist about Christmas, I realise that for us in our century Christmas is largely concerned with the ritual of coming home. This may explain the growth in the importance of Christmas over the last 150 years. We remember that Quakers traditionally did not celebrate Christmas and neither did Congregationalists and others of the Puritan tradition until about 150 years ago. But in the 20th century we have become an increasingly rootless society, with people constantly moving about the country and with children and grandchildren scattered about. So Christmas stands for coming home, with the fireside and hearth symbolising security and stability in a most unstable world. I think of this in relation to Jesus, for during his adult time of ministry he was also a wanderer, dependent on those who took him in for food and lodging. And not only did he begin his life in the stable of an inn, but his last celebration of the Passover feast was in the upper room of an inn. Today, he is still a wanderer, except insofar as he finds a home in us now, as then.

[15 December 1985]

I've been watching the sunlight on the carpet for the past half hour. It was in the centre, but it kept moving, and now it's on Howard's shoe. You can't stop the sunlight. It keeps on moving. The light is always on the move.

I've been thinking about the symbols we've been talking about that we think bear our witness. Symbols on the walls or around our necks that tell who we are and that we think carry our message for us. They're husks, dead husks. They're where the sun was, and we tried to hold on to it. Janet was right about letting our lives speak. We speak with what we *really* are and with what we do. I had an opportunity to do a little witnessing this week, but I let it go. It would have been words and dead symbols. A student asked me if I was a Catholic. I said no; he said he thought maybe I was from the way I talked, then he asked me what religion I was. I wouldn't tell him; I said I thought a teacher should hold on to his mystique. I guess I was a little flattered to have him think that I was anything as specific and God-dazzled as a Catholic.

I think that about the best witnessing I did in that class all semester was when I read them a poem. It was 'The Waking' by Theodore Roethke, and it doesn't have any obviously religious language or symbols in it, but I think it's filled with the spirit. It's about learning where you have to go by going there: "I learn by going where I have to go." All the going I ever learned I learned by going there.

If I can use a merchandising metaphor for a moment, before you can sell something, you have to have a product. A product that you believe in. I wonder if we have anything the world would want. I think other people's handshakes are just as warm as ours. I think a lot of people are happy in their own churches and better off there than with us. There's a lot of lukewarmness with Friends and with me, and self-doubt, and I don't know how anxious I am to share that. When I think about what we have that some other churches don't have and that I believe in and that I would want to share, I think of what Anne was saying about our Peace and Service Committee's work. I think about the peace testimony. Whenever I've gotten sufficiently aroused to go out on the streets and push leaflets at people, it's been because of our peace testimony. I've pushed a few thousand of them, and the one I pushed the most of was one I wrote: it was about the symbolism of the colour white, and about how in 1971 in Vietnam it was the colour of death and also the colour of our blank signs, which we were holding in silence in front of the White House. A lot of meetings have a tradition of holding a silent peace vigil on Saturdays. Albany Meeting has carried one on for years, and I remember participating in the one Purchase Quarter used to carry on during the war. That's the kind of outreach that makes people turn to Friends as people with something worth listening to. When there's a war on and we believe passionately in its wrongness, we get up on our feet and do something to bring the message. Sitting here, looking at the sun, which is almost gone by now from where I'm looking, I can't hold on to it, and now it's gone, before I finish talking. Talking.

[22 November 1987]

* * *

I'm thinking of cranberries. They're red and they're sour. They're strung on a string around a Christmas tree. The birds are pecking at them. The tree is outside. It's a living tree, reaching into its roots, hunkering down for winter. There's no snow yet, and the ground is muddy. I don't know that I'm ready for Christmas yet. But it will come.

[13 December 1987]

* * *

Walking in the light is precarious business at best. It's a little like walking on the water. We can sit in our boat and say "Every day in every way I get better and better" and then step out onto the water and hope we don't sink. After all, we could walk on the water if we had the right equipment. Valleys have been raised up and hills laid low, by bulldozers. I think of us stepping out onto the water with our frog feet, blown-up bladders, on which we go plopping across the water – plop, plop, plop – until we get thrown off balance and fall on our faces. I remember something about an inlet from the sea in the George Fox country on which people could walk on water if they were skillful and quick. When the tide went out it was possible to ride across the shallow water on horseback, or maybe it was walking, being held up by the ground that was hidden below the surface, and cut off miles of a journey, if one didn't get careless and get caught by the incoming tide. If there is any ground for optimism, it is that there are laws in nature that we can count on to bear us up if we learn them. We don't have to build our house on shifting sands. Walking in the light, it seems to me, always involves taking a risk, because it means stepping out from the conventional wisdoms and trying to find what will bear us up in the region of the unknown. But the light keeps moving, and it is hard to place our feet in it, unless we can catch the rhythms of this dance of life.

[31 January 1988]

*   *   *

When I hear from someone an unintelligible noise or even just words that sound strange or disagreeable to me, I hope that I might have the grace to turn to that person [as Ann Saxton just had to the child who was crying as she gave her message] and say "I agree with you, Friend." Not agree on a verbal level, but agree down under, where the feelings are. "What is the sound of one hand clapping?" runs the old Zen paradox. The sound of silence, of course. We know that sound. "What is the light of darkness?" I have asked myself. Once I saw Helen Keller, just a few feet away from me at a college commencement. What astonished me was the radiance that came from her face. Her eyes were what especially struck me. I knew that she could not see anything of what I saw with my eyes. But her eyes blazed with light as she eagerly leaned forward, like me, into the dark. And I knew that I had felt a little touch of divinity in the night.

[2 December 1990]

Our national leaders and the press have been telling us that we have kicked the Vietnam syndrome, that we can all stand tall again. Everyone talks these days about pride as if it were a good thing. But for many centuries, pride was considered a sin. As it says in Corinthians, "Love suffers long and is kind; it is not puffed up." It does not boast. Yet, I know that self-confidence is necessary for being and doing our best. This has made me ask the question, what is the difference between pride and self-confidence? Pride is competitive. It measures against others, by how successful we are in beating others, pushing them around, controlling them. But we acquire self-confidence by controlling ourselves, doing what we feel we should, doing God's will. As St Paul says, "I know whom I have believed and am persuaded that he is able." And thus, we learn that we are able.

[17 March 1991]

* * *

There is a spirit that I feel here that is very quiet and very warm. I did not bring it with me. I did not expect to find it here. It seems to come up out of the floor. I did nothing to earn it. I did not say words to invoke it. I do not feel that it is something in me. It seems to be something that broods over the group, something outside us that broods over us. I do not give it a name, being somewhat cautious of names.

[28 July 1991]

* * *

Tom is right. Poughkeepsie Meeting has been going through a transition for quite a few years. I have been conscious of the stages. Perhaps not everything that has happened has been positive, but I think that when we look back on things from the perspective of four or five years from now we will see that there has been a direction that is positive. The direction is from reliance on our merely human strength and machinery to reliance on the Light.

We know its source, and as we throw ourselves into the Light more unreservedly, it will lift us up.

[10 October 1991]

* * *

I remember learning how to swim. I was seven or eight years old, and it was in a class at the local pool. Now I knew that the water was the enemy. I'd had water up my nose and down my windpipe and I knew that it hurt. I knew that the water could kill you. I knew that you had to fight the water and flail your arms around a lot or it would get you. But when I got in the class, that wasn't what they taught you. First we had to make friends with the water. We put our heads under and held our breath for a long time. Then we learned to relax in the water, just letting our arms and legs go limp with our faces down and doing the jellyfish float. Then finally they taught us to lie back on the water with our faces up and just wave our arms and legs lazily and you could just float there and the water wouldn't take you down. And it worked. The water would hold you up. There's a lesson in this. As we jump off our personal and corporate docks, as we give ourselves more and more unreservedly to the Light, it will lift us up.

[13 October 1991]

* * *

I have been thinking about knowing the Spirit in our hearts. I don't think of God as something outside us, like the principal of the school who gives us a diploma for being good and doing our work well. Rather I think of God as something in the work itself, something motivating us to do it and guiding us and making us feel a pleasure in doing it. Last night I was feeling a certain spot of joy, and as I reflected on it I thought of the joy as a kind of tune that God was playing on me as an instrument. I thought about the relationship between the music and the instrument and realised that there would be no music without the instrument, that God was REALising a pleasure in and through me, that God needs the world as much as the world needs God. We really can't separate the two, except as a way of thinking. I think we're like the leaves on the trees in the forest, shaking in the wind, and rustling. God's voice is in that, as well as in us, and there is pleasure in it: God's pleasure. I think God really loves BEing. When we say God loves us, or we love God, it's not like something outside of us, as if we were two people. It's like the pressure of the seed inside the acorn, pressing outward.

[24 November 1991]

* * *

We are all leaves on a tree. We are connected by invisible stems. The sap is running. We silently drink in light.

[February 1992]

* * *

There are two kinds of God that will probably fail you. There are doubtless others, but these are the ones that occur to me at the moment.

The first is the taskmaster God. No matter how much we do, there always seems to be more to be done to appease this God. The more we do, the more diminished we feel. We end up worn out by all our good deeds. This God is perhaps a projection of our own guilt feelings, our feelings of inadequacy. There is some valid basis for this conception of God, for we are indeed called to account for moral effort and moral standards by our experience of the divine within.

The other kind of God is what I might call the 'Santa Claus' or the 'Sugar Daddy'. Again, there is some truth in this, for God is indeed the origin of all that is good and true and just and honest and of good report, and we will probably find many good things in our lives when we are in tune with the divine wavelength. But to expect a positive response to every petition in prayer, to regard God as a dispenser of patronage to those who have 'voted right' is unrealistic and sure to lead to disappointment and disillusion.

God is neither of these, and both of them, and more. I think of Theodore Roethke's line about being entertained sometimes by the spirit. Sometimes, not always. Sometimes we have been entertained by the spirit, have been welcomed into that dwelling where all is alive and filled with light.

[15 March 1992]

* * *

Every now and then we take the old car in for a tune-up. The pitted plugs get replaced, the wires and the distributor are checked to make sure the spark is getting through, the idle is adjusted so we don't stall out when resting, or waste energy racing at stop lights. And the dwell is adjusted. I don't know what dwell is, but I like to think of "dwell in the house of the Lord forever." And then, when everything is purring, we can take the old jalopy out for a spin. We all need a regular tune-up. My mother told me once of a man who thought that all you had to do to a car was put the gas in. We won't get far with that philosophy before we wear out and break down. It takes attention and work if we are to

see

love

do.

[22 March 1992]

* * *

I'm thinking of ground water. Not the kind that runs down the road after a rain or that stands muddy in pools. I'm thinking of the water that comes out of my well by the driveway. It comes from about 60 or 70 feet down, and it comes out sparkling and clear after being filtered through all the rocks. The amazing thing is that after going through all that dirt, it comes out clear. Here in meeting I feel as if something like that water was settling in, being filtered out, going through the cracks and crevices, pulled by something like gravity toward the Centre. It's the still water to be led beside, to restore the soul.

[6 September 1992]

* * *

In a meeting for worship there are two processes going on that seem like exact opposites. I haven't decided whether they are going on simultaneously or alternately. I'm referring to settling down and stirring up. I think of one of those glass globes with the artificial snow inside. You shake the globe and the snow swirls up into the water and drifts around and gradually settles down. You stir it up again, and again the swirl and the drifting and the settling out. We see this process in a lot of places. In muddy water the particles gradually settle down to the bottom. We walk into a room and the dust motes are stirred up and dance around in the sunbeams that come through the southern windows, then they gradually settle down and the sunbeams are clear again. A meeting for worship is like that: we're thinking about what we're going to do tomorrow and what we did yesterday, or about problems and ideas, and then gradually those things settle out and we experience perhaps what Jesus meant when he said "My peace I give unto you". And when we experience that peace, our minds are integrated and experience oneness, sometimes referred to as wholeness. All the filings under the magnetic pull turn in one direction.

And then there's the stirring up. I visualise electrons torn off by a generator and streaming through a wire, colliding and sending the pulse along, making light, making heat, making motors go round. There is a great circularity to the universe. Power goes around in circles. Things go up and things go down. A meeting is a mighty generator of power, and it stirs us up to do things. Perhaps it stirs us most when the bumping confusion of things has settled out and we are integrated, whole, our inner selves sorted out and the atoms facing in one direction, one polarity. *Sursum corda*, lift up your hearts, is the ritual exhortation. And in that upliftedness we go around and down and find the root which is the source of all power.

[17 January 1993]

* * *

You have to sift through a lot of ore to find one jewel.

Right now, I am holding in my hand a polished stone. It is about one inch long and three-fourths of an inch wide. It is flat on one side and humped on the other. With a little imagination you could say it looks like a heart. It's not cut to any shape: it's a natural stone. It's deep reddish and brown and has veins running through it. Viola gave it to me two days ago as an anniversary present. She knew it was the one thing I wanted, because she had showed me a stone just like it that she was planning to give to her grandson. I told her about Henry Ward Beecher, who carried jewels in his pocket to finger. That was the whole idea: a stone to carry in my pocket.

I've been thinking about the differences between my pet rock and a diamond. A diamond would have hard edges and a sharp point and wouldn't be comfortable and smooth and warm like this. It wouldn't have this deep red colour. A diamond this big would be very valuable. I'd be afraid of losing it. I'd be afraid someone would steal it. I wouldn't feel comfortable carrying it around. It wouldn't be friendly and warm. Its value would be objective and could be passed on from generation to generation. My stone has value only to me. It has value only because of who gave it to me.

You have to sift through a lot of ore to find your one jewel.

[18 April 1993]

* * *

Somehow, if you stand steady long enough, your feet will strike roots into the ground, and out of the ground will come a strength more than your own.

[9 May 1993]

* * *

You must try on all the garments of God until you find the one that fits you. And then you must move in it. At first it may feel a little strange, because it is new and different, but as you move in it you will find that along with the new responsibilities comes an enlarged sense of freedom.

[19 September 1993]

*　*　*

I received a telephone call from God, but all he got was an answering-machine message saying that I was busy, that I was out. There are so many ways that I have of putting a wall between myself and God, of being busy.

I'm reminded of when my 15-year-old grandson visited me two months ago. It was difficult to communicate with him: I couldn't get through. He had his headphones on or he had the music up so loud that I couldn't talk to him very much. I sat with him and listened to his music carefully and asked him about what the lyrics meant, but most of the time he seemed to have a wall around him. He was having trouble communicating not just with me but with his parents and with his school, and I suspect with himself. And God? Forget it. But I'm afraid I have my own headphones on.

Thirty years ago I read about the double search, in which we try to find God and God tries to find us. I haven't thought about that idea for even five minutes until now. When I started in meeting this morning I went through a routine, trying to make contact with God, but I can't say that I was really getting through. Then, when I stopped trying and was just letting my mind go into neutral, I saw something a little like light out of nowhere.

For thousands of years Christians have been arguing about the relative merits of activity and passivity in communication with God. I don't have any answer to that question for right now, but I'm going to explore the possibility that it takes a little of both. Putting a little space in our lives is one way of making sure that when God calls the phone will be back on the hook.

[17 October 1993]

The test is where we turn when we're in trouble. Some people turn their faces to the wall and give up. They want to die. Some turn to distractions: drink or drugs or the various dissipations. Those who turn to the Lord will renew their strength. They will mount up with wings as the eagles; they will run and not be weary; they will walk and not faint. I have often heard it said that this is a strange anticlimax. But it's the order of things as I think we experience them in the life cycle. In the first flush of youthful enthusiasm as we experience God we mount up with wings; we feel we're flying. Then we rush around, busily doing things for the King; we run, and we're not weary. But as we get older we slow down. We take our time. We still do things, but not as fast. We walk. We relax into the comfort and security of Presence.

[31 October 1993]

*　*　*

We all feel the gift of life within us. It's all we have. We don't know where it came from. We don't know how long we'll have it. Nothing seems to stop it. The moss keeps pushing up between the cracks. The leaves keep coming back. Everywhere we see the gift misused, disrespected. But we seek to cherish it. We seek to nurture it. We seek to be a perfect receptacle for it. To become a cup to receive the divine water and let it overflow.

[7 November 1993]

*　*　*

This is the brittle season. We easily snap and crack. The ice on the tree branches cracks, falls off, and rattles on the snow crust. It catches the sun and sparkles. When we face the sun we transmit light. In our brokenness if we face the sun we become witnesses to the light.

[27 February 1994]

*　*　*

I am struck by the fact that Jesus did not write a book. The founders and explicators of other religions wrote books. Muhammad wrote a book. Joseph Smith wrote a book, or found one dictated by an angel. Mary Baker Eddy wrote a book. St Thomas Aquinas wrote a book and answered all the questions, to form a 'perfect' system of theology. But Jesus did not write a book, something frozen in stone that could be his final and complete and perfect words, his system. Instead, he trusted his words to the uncertain memories of his disciples, sent them forth on the stream of memory to lodge as they would, like seeds, waiting to sprout. Quakers testify to the profound openness, perhaps even the uncertainty, of religion, its principles living, not frozen, waiting to grow in each one of us. A few minutes ago a picture came into my mind out of nowhere. It was of a sheet of music, a hymn. The first line was written out. The second line had one bar of music; the rest was blank. The third line had one bar written out; the rest was blank. The fourth line was the same: one bar and the rest blank, waiting to be filled in by the singer. Religion is always a launching forth into the unknown.

[10 April 1994]

* * *

I am amazed at the persistence of life which keeps on looking for the fountain, the fountain in the rocks that has dried up months ago and won't be renewed until spring. I watch the deer walking along the mountain, past my window, nibbling the new shoots in the spring. All winter I saw those same deer go past my window, floundering in the snow, and I wondered what was keeping them alive. They had long ago eaten the hemlocks as high as they could reach. Months earlier they had eaten up the last leaves on the shrubs around my house, as high as they could reach. Then the spring came and the deer were still there.

They say you have to know darkness before you can appreciate light. This seems to me true both symbolically and literally. If I were living in a desert with no shade, no shadows, and if night never came for relief, I think I would hate the light. I sit here with my eyes closed, so that I can become sensitive to the invisible vibrations that emanate from each person, see the light that is only visible through darkness.

[14 May 1994]

*   *   *

[Al Bahret, who had just been welcomed into membership, had quoted from Shakespeare's sonnets 29 and 30, changing "dear friend" to "dear Friends".]

The phrase 'dear friend' has a special significance for me. It's the title of a song from a musical, *She Loves Me*, that I have played many times, and it's the only musical that I ever took my children to. 'Dear Friend' is sung by the man and woman leads as they write letters back and forth to each other, each at a desk on opposite sides of the stage. They have never met; they don't even know each other's names. They fall in love, still not knowing each other's names, and finally they meet. And they find that they know each other. They've been working side by side in a store all along, and the irony is that they had been having conflict with each other in this 'real' life. Of course, they fall in love, for real now, in 'real' life.

I'm thinking of that as an analogy to our relationship with God. We haven't seen God. We correspond with him at a distance. Then we make a discovery: we realise that God is in the people we've known all along. They may even be people we've been in conflict with. We discover who these people really are. We discover that the ideal Love who was held at a distance from us, in a merely letter-writing relationship, is in people. Everything becomes transformed. Now we really know God. Before, it was just a long-distance telephone call. And so I say to Al "Dear Friend."

[21 May 1994]

*   *   *

I started out thinking about a line from Wordsworth about "an eye made quiet by the power of harmony, and the deep power of joy."

I was thinking about that because Peter's here, and I know that it's one of his favourite lines. That expresses what we're looking for here in our Friends meeting: harmony and peace, a release from restlessness. Then I thought about a song, a rock and roll song, that my son wrote, that starts out with the lines "My heart was clapping out the beat / As we were dancing in the heat." That made me think about varieties of worship. If we were in a different place of worship, say a Black church in rural Mississippi, we might be clapping out the beat right now, and that too would be valid, an expression of "the power of harmony, and the deep power of joy."

A couple of months ago as I was walking into my American literature class, the young woman walking ahead of me had the headphones on and I could hear the rock beat coming out of the headphones. I commented on how it sounded good, and she handed me the headphones and asked if I wanted to hear it. I stood in front of the class and listened, and then I opened up my textbook to that day's assignment, which was Thoreau's *Walden*. I started reading to them with the headphones still on. I read them the famous passage about silence and solitude and about what a delicious evening it is "when the whole body is one sense and imbibes delight through every pore", and I read the passage in time with the beat that the headphones were clapping out. The kids loved it and so did I, and that was a real rocking and rolling class.

We live in a restless age, when things are speeding up, and there isn't much tolerance for sitting still and being quiet. The whole direction of our age is going counter to Quakerism and its emphasis on finding the still centre. Television is speeding up and the blips in the commercials are getting shorter and shorter. The culture is full of glitz and jumpiness and things happening in a bounce. That's entertainment. In Quaker worship there isn't any entertainment, there isn't even anything happening if we don't find it happening inside us.

I think about when I was 11, 12, 13 years old. We all played football on corner lots and lawns in front of the churches. Sometimes it was touch football, but mostly it was tackle. The rich kids and the lucky ones had helmets, most of us didn't. It was disorganised, but we had fun. We played every day after school. I remember that sometimes, after everyone else had left, my best friend and I would keep on playing until dark, just picking up the ball and running and tackling. I don't see much of that on the corner lots and church lawns anymore. I guess the kids must be inside watching football on television or maybe playing on organised school teams with proper equipment. Why play the game poorly when anytime you want to you can see it played well, professionally, the way it's really supposed to be played?

I guess Quaker worship is a little like that sandlot football – not very professional, not with all the right moves. Maybe it isn't very much, and we're certainly not very many – but it's ours.

[29 May 1994]

* * *

In the first stage of worship I descended into sleep and hung there, suspended in the dark. In the second stage I floated in the darkness, rocking, like a boat taking the tide. In the third stage there was light moving out of the darkness, over the face of the waters, as in the Beginning. In the fourth stage I became conscious of my body, pressing against the chair, and of people around me in the circle. The clock whirred, time started. It was time to Begin.

[Summer 1994]

We give each other our spark, and if it comes from the pure source it will light a flame.

[undated, 1994]

* * *

God is in the silence and God is in the noise. We make the noise into music, and the music is full of silences. [Al Bahret had commented on the fact that he could hear the noise made by the fluorescent lights, and it was distracting.]

[September 1994]

* * *

The world is full of tribulation. People are sick; people are dying. Our houses are decaying: the foundations are rotting, our roofs are caving in, our rooms are a mess and our budgets are untidy. Jesus said "In this world you have tribulation, but be of good cheer, for I have overcome the world." The lines that Viola quoted from the New Testament about "the time is come and now is when ye shall worship him in spirit and in truth" are, if I remember correctly, from the story about the woman at the well. There, Jesus speaks of a well of water "springing up into everlasting life." I visualise us here in our circle, gathered around a pool, a deep pool of water. We look down into the water. It is pure and clear but dark. A lotus blossom rises up out of the water and opens. Its petals expand and stretch out and touch each one of us, and we become calm. In the centre is our peace. Around the edge of our circle, behind us, is a turbulence: all the things of this world that clamour for our attention. [At this point there was a rustling as the children came in and then became quiet.] The rustling around us and inside us quiets. We drop our coin into the fountain – and we drink of the water.

[4 November 1994]

* * *

I have to quiet the many voices within me, to hear the one true voice. Except it's not a voice. It's a fountain of light. And not white light either. Coloured lights. Not strong primary colours, blue and red and yellow. Not the peacock's tail. Muted colours, a fountain of soft, muted colours. There is so much between me and that.

Suppose, for example, I'm 40 again. Dante wrote that midway in the journey of his life he found himself in a pathless wood. Dreary and dark. Then he found a guide who took him through the nine circles of Hell, the nine circles of Purgatory, and finally the nine circles of Heaven, where at last he saw the angels swirling like a fountain of light around the Centre, which was God. He organised his way out of the pathless wood and centred his life around an Authority.

But I tend to look to a less external authority. Lao Tse in the *Tao Te Ching* wrote it this way: he said that better than listening to the tinkling of jade pendants was to hear the rock growing in the cliffs. The tinkling of jade pendants stands for all the trivia that floods my life, the television, or even the deeper concerns that the newspaper brings. There, I'm in the time-battered world, frazzled. But to hear the rocks growing in the cliffs we would have to enter into the mind of God. There, millennia are a wink of the eye. To float on a sea of the centuries. To imagine eternity. That's why we're here.

[22 January 1995]

* * *

This room yesterday was full of numbers when the Financial Services Committee was meeting here. So I'd like to talk about exponents. An exponent is a person devoted to a philosophy or a religion, who exemplifies it and talks about it to others. But then we also have mathematical exponents. An exponent raises a number to a higher power. X squared, x to the third power, x to the fourth power. X to the fourth, that's a whole lot.

And a person is raised to a higher power by the exponentiality of what's out there and in here. I think when we're operated upon by a higher power, we're lifted up and become more than ourselves. But this power is also within us.

This morning I read an article by a professor at Harvard Medical School. It is about a power that he said is within every person – the power of relaxation, which we can unlock by a simple technique. The article tells about all the good physical results of such relaxing – better heart, better general health, better sleep. The technique is as simple as counting. One, one, one, as we breathe in and out. Or any other word will do. It can be 'peace' or 'love', or anything like that; the important thing is to keep the rhythm going. And the professor says that visualising a peaceful scene, like a lake or clouds, will also help. (As I thought about that, I saw a whole room full of integers – one, one, one – floating out of my mouth.) The point is that this relaxation response, this power is in everybody – it's natural, it's just there.

A few moments ago I felt something come into me that was very relaxing and very energising and that brought me and my wandering thoughts to attention. I often feel it here, and I guess it's why I come. It didn't seem to come from inside me. I had a sense that it was coming from outside me. I've often thought that there's someone here, I don't know who, who is a secret spiritual friend, whose communion with some force is breaking through and being shared with me. It's as if the ripples flowing from that person flowed outward and touched the ripples flowing from me, and were joined in a lake of light.

I remember our Powell House retreat last October. We heard the story about the five aged monks who were told by a rabbi that the Messiah was one of them. They began to wonder. And as they wondered which one of them it was, each treated the others with new respect. And the respect – call it love – started to ripple and spread. Other people were drawn to them and to the attracting force radiating from the monastery. The dying monastery was reborn, renewed, as new monks flocked to it. It's like that in us. The secret friend is really there. The potential, exponential power is really there. Outside. Inside. In everyone. You doubt this, of course. But try saying that with each slow breath. Outside. Inside. In everyone. It becomes true as we enact it.

[17 September 1995]

* * *

There is an astonishing stillness in this room. I feel that the stillness is greater than if I were here alone. I think a lot of people come to this room as refugees – refugees from a world of blast and blare, refugees from a world where ideas are pushed at them by inflexible people who have lost their pliancy. In this quiet place people have space to grow, to become themselves. This is a very spacious place.

[24 September 1995]

* * *

The flowers opened in the spring. But that was expected. You were looking forward to it. The leaves descended in the autumn wind, and you felt sad. But that was expected. You will be surprised when God breaks in from a place where you were not looking, when you discover an unexpected depth in someone you scarcely knew. When this happens reach out, reach out, palm upward, and warm your hand.

[12 November 1995]

* * *

"The Word was made flesh" is an odd statement if you stop to think about it. But of course we've heard it so many times that it's become one of those warm fuzzies that we don't think about, a teddy bear to hold onto.

What's odd about "the Word was made flesh" is that it seems to be backwards. First come the people, we think, and then they make the words. Isn't this the way the whole world is? The physical world is primary, is what supports and houses our occasional flirtations with the spiritual part of our being. The idea that the spiritual could produce the physical seems strange to anyone who has grown up in the modern world, where so many scientists have been busily questioning whether there is anything such as spirit at all – that is to say, anything more than the electricity that travels along the wires of our nervous system.

But we are told in the Gospel of John that "the Word was made flesh." Of course, we can once again domesticate all the strangeness and dismiss it from our minds by saying that John is talking about

Jesus Christ and the Logos and that this statement has nothing to do with us.

But that it has a lot to do with us became a bit more evident to me today when I was playing with the bell-ringers, facing them. I saw rosy faces. They were alive, totally involved with the experience of shared creation. And this new creation, this roseate flesh, started with Idea, with musical ideas in the minds of Mozart and the composers of 'Silent Night' and '*Dona Nobis Pacem*'. After centuries, the ideas survive in the form of marks on paper, marks on paper that become living in us.

What I have just been saying to you lay in my mind for several minutes, inert, merely ideas and therefore not worth sharing with you. But then I focused on a dark shape deep inside me, and the words became real and something I wanted to share. The Word becomes real when it really enters into us.

[10 December 1995]

* * *

Unless you touch me, Lord, I cannot burn.

Something that is chemically inert cannot enter into a chemical reaction. Dirt, for example, cannot burn.

Christmas is a pageant, one about the transformation of inert elements into life. The pageant aspect of it is sometimes a bit of a problem for some of us, when we feel the artificial, material aspect of it negating the spiritual significance. The Christmas tree glows and sparkles, but we know that at the end it will be taken out, needles falling and upside down, to be dumped on the refuse heap. We are afraid that this is the truth about us, that we are only physical bodies, mechanical dolls, after all.

Yesterday I went to *The Nutcracker* ballet at the Bardavon with Viola's family, including three of her grandchildren. It was the first time I had ever seen the whole ballet. The plot revolved around a magician who made life-sized dolls. When he took them out of the box and wound them up they danced, like real human beings. I was fascinated by the multiple layers: here were real people who acted like dolls, who acted like real people, and who then went back to acting like dolls. Their dance over, they stiffened and bent; then men came in and carried them offstage, upside down, like so many pieces of wood. It was funny, and yet profound. We were reminded that a lot of the Christmas pageant is artificial, a matter of mechanical dolls and toy soldiers and stuffed animals.

But what it is really about is transformation, about the ability of the seemingly inert, the material world, to become living, to burn with life. We sit here in our circle, not inert elements. Each one of us is a candle, with the potential to be touched into flame. Maybe the fire will touch us this time, maybe it will not. But unless you touch me, Lord, I cannot burn.

[17 December 1995]

* * *

Each of us comes here each week hoping for a blessed moment. It need not be much – perhaps a moistened eye, a touch on our shoulder, like the touch of a hand, a feeling of clarity at the centre of the mind, a warmth and intensity in the chest, or a sense of electricity travelling around the circle. To find it we have to sift down through a lot of thoughts and notions, perhaps reaching a place of emptiness and darkness. But if we can find our blessed moment, we can lay aside the triviality and trash of everyday; we can move onward with assurance, and know that we are real.

[31 December 1995]

* * *

I am sure that the Christians in Bosnia think that they're doing the will of God. I am equally sure that the Muslims in Bosnia think that they're doing the will of God. And I don't think that either one is doing the will of God. All of which leaves the whole matter of the will of God in a state of considerable confusion.

Now I don't put forth what I am about to say as any kind of

revealed truth. I might change my mind tomorrow and say the opposite. But I think that the concept of 'good' applies only to humans. Good is what *we* want. For example, this week I read in *The New York Times* science section about the Australian redback spider and the black widow spider. When these spiders have sex the female eats the male. In fact the redback male offers himself to the female by doing a complex somersault during copulation that places his most appetising parts squarely in front of the female's jaws. She obliges by eating him while he continues to enjoy himself in connection with her at both ends. What a way to go! And the kicker on this is that this process gives red spiders a positive evolutionary advantage in survival of the species. The self-sacrifice of the male ensures that the female will get a good meal and lay more eggs. Evil – or good?

Or again: this week I've been thinking about ice. I look out my window and see huge icicles hanging from the rain gutters and gleaming in the sun. They're beautiful, so beautiful that I got my camera out and shot some pictures of them. But right after I took the pictures I knocked the icicles off to relieve the weight on the gutters. And the icicles over my door were a sharp-pointed menace ready to fall off and spear someone walking through the door. Last week I saw huge icicles hanging from an electric wire right over the path from our parking lot. They were spectacular, but I knocked them down. And on our roof, the water creeps up under the slates and then freezes and lifts the slates, and then we get the leaks coming through our ceiling that you see over there in the corner. Ice: beautiful or menace?

When I came into the room just now I listened for the drips. I had been hearing them in the room for three days. The non-drips this morning were music to my ears. They made a silence so profound that they drowned all discourse.

What are the sounds of silence? When John Woolman visited the Indians on the frontier on a peace mission in wartime, he didn't speak their language. But the story is that they understood something of each other anyway, because they were united in the place where the words come from.

Which brings us back to the Bosnians, Christian and Muslim. Is it possible that they are united in "the place where the words come from?"

[14 January 1996]

* * *

Quakerism, like Christianity, believes that God is seeable. The other half of the paradox is the belief that God is invisible, not to be made into graven images, not to be worshipped in idols. Christians believe that God was made flesh and dwelt among us, that we have heard God in words. Quakers speak of God manifested in human actions and manifest in the wonders of nature. We see through a glass darkly, but St Paul says there is a time and a dimension in which we shall see face to face. I have not wanted to believe in a visible God, so I ask myself what this all means.

We could turn it around. What does God see? The Divine Spirit looks out upon the world, seeing as in a mirror, and sees a reflection of itself. Everywhere, the divine spirit is manifested, high and lifted up. When we look upon the visible world and enter into it in its own inner spirit, we too are exalted, high and lifted up. We hear a singing, a harmony of many voices, sometimes discordant, sometimes sweet, but nonetheless marvellous. Between human beings and the Divine Spirit, I see the surface of that mirror in which dances a mutual reflection.

Yesterday I saw the opera *Falstaff*. The concluding chorus astonished me, it was so different from anything else Verdi wrote, so different indeed from anything I had ever heard in an opera. The whole cast and chorus came forward to the front of the stage, facing the audience; the children sat on the edge of the stage swinging their legs. The notes tumbled out in what seemed a swirling confusion of everyone singing something different all at once, yet all mingling so precisely, turning and turning inward upon itself and swirling outward again in an astonishing fugue structure such as Bach might have written. And what I felt was that singers and audience were facing each other as in a mirror, reflecting each other, caught up in that grand fugue, lighting each other's faces. It seemed that in a mirror of light and sound, audience and singers were turning each other on, in an act of mutual applause. It was a tumbling movement of sound and light, and yet here was a world in process of creation. The world in process of creation is always at risk, and yet somehow underneath it is something solid and stable and secure. Call it process itself. Call it God.

What a wonderful world our God has made for us. How exciting it has been for God!

[4 February 1996]

*　*　*

'The fear of God' means for some people respect or reverence for God. But there is another sense in which we really are afraid of God, and I'm not referring to the old fear of Hell.

When you've been close to the fire, you know that it can burn you as well as warm you.

[9 February 1996]

*　*　*

It's me, it's me, it's me, O Lord, standing in the need of prayer. Sometimes it's harder to forgive ourselves than it is to forgive others.

Christians over the centuries have developed a very elaborate set of ideas about forgiveness, about the need for it, and about its source. But concepts and doctrines don't do us much good when we wrestle existentially with real life, with the problem of reconciling justice and mercy in real situations.

Jesus presents us with a paradox. On the one hand he says "Be ye therefore perfect, even as your Father which is in heaven is perfect." On the other hand he says "Come unto me, all ye that labour and are heavy laden, and I will give you rest." On the one hand we are presented with the demand, impossible of fulfilment, that drives us into guilt. On the other hand we are told that all our strivings can cease, that we can rest in him.

We are stretched on the rack – but not to break.

Your tears are the true sign of your acceptance.

[11 February 1996]

* * *

The saints speak of the pure light. By this I suppose they mean a light that is not crossed by conflict or sullied by self. We are all like blind persons, groping toward the light. In my own experience, in meeting, I don't go directly to the light. I go to it through darkness. I don't want you to moralise this, as if by darkness I meant evil and by light I meant good. I am speaking of something direct, visual, not an abstraction.

Some poet speaks of "darkness visible", a light shining in darkness and through darkness. I think about that blind person. What would light be like to a blind person? John Milton, who had lost his once-good eyesight, wrote in *Paradise Lost*, book 3, of what the light meant to him: "Hail holy light, offspring of heaven's first beam; or of the eternal co-eternal beam may I express thee unblamed." And all of *Paradise Lost* is filled with that darkness visible, that light that filled the imagination of the poet who was himself blind but full of the remnants of what he had once seen and full of the presence of what he now experienced. Henry James writes in *The Golden Bowl* of what it would be like to experience a garden in the dark, just before the dawn, not to see it but to feel all the flowers opening, leaning toward the light that was to come. Such flowers would be like a light in the darkness, a perfume, one that made "the whole air its medium."

I once experienced the light as seen by a blind person. The person was Helen Keller. She was coming toward me after receiving an honorary degree, up the steps of the library. She passed me, not ten feet away, and I saw her face very clearly. She was leaning forward, expectantly, leaning into the light. She pushed the light ahead of her like a wave. Her face was filled with something I can only call joy. Everything had been taken away from her but life itself, and by life itself her face was filled with joy. In that moment, which was only a flash, I saw darkness visible.

Would that we could all be connected with that force from underground that flows upward, into the very fibres of ourselves.

[31 March 1996]

* * *

Each breath that we take is from a very large reservoir. There is enough to go around. We need a theology of abundance. There is enough love in the universe to go around. The old theology was a theology of scarcity: God rewarded those who deserved it and punished those who didn't measure up. But there is a heart at the centre of reality. We live in a world that was born, not made. We breathe in that life with each breath.

[26 May 1996]

* * *

I didn't know what 'praising God' meant until two days ago when I read a passage from Alice Walker's *The Colour Purple*. The idea of praising God didn't appeal to me because it seemed to make God out to be some egotistical being. But Alice Walker says that God loves admiration. She goes on to say that God doesn't like it "if you walk by the colour purple in a field somewhere and don't notice it." What is important then is responding, really appreciating the beauty in the world. But it shouldn't take a beautiful spring day like this one before we see beauty. The real test is our ability to appreciate things that we might be inclined to call ugly. That's what the movie *Beauty and the Beast* is all about. Beauty had to love the horrible beast before he could turn into the handsome prince. When I was a sophomore in college my dormitory building was still under construction. Right outside my window was a pile of junk: boards and stuff. At first I saw only the ugliness, but then one day it suddenly looked beautiful to me. The difference between a religious and a secular view of the world: a religious view can find the beauty hidden inside even the ugly. And that's what praising God means to me.

[2 June 1996]

* * *

When you say "good morning" and really feel it, it exerts transforming power. You remember Maya Angelou, who read the poem at the inauguration in 1993. The last line of the poem, standing out all by itself, was a simple and surprising "good morning", and the way she said it was so refreshing that it caught the attention of the whole country. There was a lot behind that "good morning". Maya Angelou wrote a book called *I Know Why the Caged Bird Sings*. I remember a passage from that book. It told about how when she was a girl a crowd of white teenagers came in to persecute and harass her at her grandmother's little store in rural Arkansas. And it told about the wisdom she got from her grandmother about how to respond to that harassment without crawling or cringing or feeling bitterness. Maya Angelou knew why the caged bird sang. She knew what "good morning" meant. When we learn to transform our pain and discouragement into joy, then we catch that little wink of heaven which is what I mean by God.

[22 September 1996]

* * *

Fear cannot overtake you if you run slower than it does.

[13 October 1996]

* * *

It's a scary thing to open yourself up to the Spirit. You might find yourself impelled to do something you really don't want to do. Or to give up something you don't want to give up. Or to stop doing something you've been in the habit of doing. That's why it's so uncomfortable to have Jesus as a member of our family. He makes such uncompromising demands. He challenges us to get out of our comfortable grooves, our ruts of passive religiosity. We haven't really crucified him. But I find myself looking the other way, a lot.

[30 March 1997 (Easter)]

* * *

God comes into a room like a beautiful woman who, when she sits down with perfect composure and exuding the perfume of her smile, casts a radiance over the room and commands the attention of everyone.

[June 1997]

* * *

Sometimes the spirit is wrought, like wrought iron, from intense struggle, and its resolution. Or sometimes the spirit comes like the dew in the night; we don't see it coming, but when we wake up in the morning it is just there, bringing freshness. However it comes, it is yours, it is the most intimate thing about you. On the other hand, you see its potential in everyone you touch. However it comes, let it come. Allow it. Allow it to come. Let it take you.

[20 July 1997]

* * *

As I was going along the Arterial this morning, driving eastward toward the sun and toward my destination at the meeting house, I passed the Roman Catholic church on the corner. Above the door was a large sign that read "Renew!". Now I knew what that meant, for "Renew!" is the message of all religions everywhere. And I also knew what it meant in that particular place and time. It was a call to renew ties to God and to the mother church, ties that had perhaps languished for a few years. It was a call to Catholics to come home.

The desire to go home is a basic part of our being. That's why, when we share our earliest memories with each other in a Claremont

Dialogue, we feel a sense of renewal. Reconnecting with roots is something that we periodically need to do. On the other hand, we want to change, to move on, to grow. These things in us are a part of the basic rhythm of nature. At this spring season especially, we want to get back to the dirt and put seed in the ground. We live in the cycle of the seasons. We plant seed, then we weed, harvest, and lie fallow, waiting for the call of another spring. We want to go home, to the way things were, and yet paradoxically we want to be renewed, all new inside, as if what was had never been.

Bill Clinton, addressing his daughter's high school commencement this week, concluded by assuring the graduates that although they would soon be making a break, entering into a new independence, "You can come home again, despite what you may have heard." But can we, really? Home will have changed, and we will have changed. We want it that way. We know that if we do not change, do not grow, we will die. Of course, we know we will die anyway, but we are optimistic and we hold on; we hope for seasons of renewal along the way that will keep us alive.

When we leave home, enter into time, and mix with the world, we get soiled. Things wear out and get dirty. Decay is a precondition of growth, part of the cycle of life. Growth is a constant process of repair and rebirth. Regularly and ritualistically we wash our faces, and regularly and ritualistically we wash our clothes. Any cleansing involves agitation. Things get shaken up and tossed around and shaken out. This is disconcerting. It produces our nostalgia, our desire to go home again. But remember: renewal always involves change as well as a return to roots. Home will never be the same again.

We drive eastward toward the sun. We know that it is also setting. We dare to live anyway, as close as possible to the edge of the unknown. There at the edge we put seed in the ground. And so it is – the only way there is – that we and the world are renewed. We come to meeting for our weekly facewash, our weekly soul-lift, hoping to renew our connection with what we have felt most deeply in the past, hoping to renew our connection with each other, hoping for some challenge, some vision that will capture us – hoping for a rebirth of our deeper selves. What we need to know is that the same Power that was there in the past is also up ahead of us, or perhaps more accurately is up above us, perhaps more accurately still is there inside us. The connection that we need to make is always available, here and now.

[June 1998]

* * *

There is no more secure basis for religion than a sense of wonder at the ordinary.

[18 October 1998]

* * *

There is no peace without patience. There is no peace without overcoming our resentments.

[undated, 1998]

* * *

Jesus came into the world for one purpose: to prove the power of love.

[undated, 1998]

* * *

Thank you consequence. Imagine a world without consequence, without cause and effect, one in which we could evade the consequences of our actions. We can imagine a world of chaos, but it's not the world we live in.

[undated, 1998]

* * *

Life is recreated every day, every hour, every minute, multitudinous as the fish in the sea, omnipresent as breathing, imperative as hunger. It is transmitted only by touch, because it has to be.

[29 November 1998]

* * *

Spreading sand on walks and driveway this morning I realised that
it takes some grit to make us go. Too much smoothness weakens us
morally, spiritually, and even physically. To build muscle, we have to
work against resistance, don't we?

[3 January 1999]

* * *

When the Holy Spirit comes into us we become exactly like a flower,
the sap coming up in us, opening us, stretching us outward, giving
us a brief beauty.

[8 August 1999]

* * *

Stay close to the Divine Centre within you. Do not let yourself be
pulled hither and thither. Do not be dazzled by the lure of success or
discouraged by the apparent lack of it. There is a tap root inside of
you that strikes deep into the soil in which true nourishment is.

[24 October 1999]

* * *

Beauty is subjective – all those things inside pressing to get out.
Beauty is objective – all those things outside clamouring to get in.
Beauty is in the union of the objective and the subjective. Beauty
is in the eye of the beholder, as the saying goes. What matters is
paying attention. It doesn't much matter what you pay attention to.
It can be a grain of dirt, an apple core, a flower, a sunset, the way
the light falls on a table, the grain of the wood, the wrinkles on an
old hand, a person. A couple of weeks ago I saw the most beautiful
sunset I had seen in fifty years. Viola and I were driving just south
of New Paltz. I pulled into a parking lot at the side of the road and

we looked at the sunset. A van pulled in beside us and did the same thing. As I watched the colours change and fade I thought about how this had been happening for millions of years. I thought about how finally there were eyes to see it and wondered what it was like before there were eyes. And then it seemed to me that God was beholding Himself in the mirror of my eyes.

[11 November 1999]

* * *

Just now, confronting the Mystery, my thoughts went first to some lines by William Wordsworth that go like this: "something far more deeply interfused, / Whose dwelling is the light of setting suns / And the round ocean and the living air / ...and in the mind of man." It was the word 'interfused' that grabbed me. Poets think in metaphors and analogies, and Wordsworth was thinking about the relation of spirit and matter. We live in a world where things are permeable that seem to be solid. Heat travels through a brick wall, for instance, though it may take a while. Radio waves go through the brick wall in an instant. We are permeable. Food and air go into us and are transformed into energy, thoughts, purposes, feelings. I speak so far of what we all know. But there is more to Mystery. We are surrounded by a golden veil. There is a golden veil between people, and when two people fall in love they see it, literally, in each other's eyes. Each of us is like a cup into which there is a flow of energy. Call it spirit. But this cup is permeable. We cannot hold on to spirit; we cannot possess it. We can only transmit it. We are permeable beings.

[16 January 2000]

* * *

This morning I saw something very beautiful. For several days I had been seeing the grey row of icicles hanging from our roof. But this morning it was different. I was washing fruit in the kitchen sink. Today there was sun, making sparks all along the edge of each icicle. But if I had merely looked at all of them I would have missed it. It was when I focused on just one icicle that I saw a large spot of light suddenly flame out along its edge. Then I looked at the spark above that and then the one above that and so on up to the top. I counted 13 flame blossoms on that one icicle. I thought about the obvious comparison with diamonds, but I had never seen so big or so brilliant a sparkle come from any diamond. Yes, diamonds are forever, and the icicle would be gone in a few days. And my moment of seeing the ice-blossoms would be gone in a second or two. But I thought of how eternity is composed of such moments, such heaped-up spots of light. Or at least that is how we know eternity here and now.

[6 February 2000]

*　*　*

One of the exciting events of my nine-year-old life was a family excursion to Mammoth Cave in Kentucky. It was summer, and there was a cool draft of air from the mouth of the cave. They said the temperature inside never changed, winter or summer.

In human beings, the self is an echoing mammoth cave. Those kept inside by guilt, by despair, by boredom, can wander endlessly. They can become acclimatised to the cave and even prefer it. This morning I was reading Franz Kafka's story 'A Hunger Artist', about a man who fasted professionally to entertain the circus crowd. Finally he starved himself to death, because, he said, there was nothing he wanted to eat. How many hunger artists are there in this world, going around in circles inside the cave, starved for food of the spirit because their five senses detect nothing they want to eat?

Plato gives us an allegory about such cave-dwellers. They have never seen daylight. The only light in the cave is the fire behind them, which casts their shadows on the wall, shadows which they take for reality. If they went outside, says Plato, the light would dazzle them and they would shrink from it. In the cave of their various forms of neurosis – guilt or despair or boredom – the hunger artists shrink from food.

They say that the definition of a human being is that we are the animal with an affinity for spirit, that we are heliotropic, attracted toward the light. I wonder. I look at the plant on the floor there in the corner. I give it a quarter turn from time to time, and by the next Sunday its leaves have turned once again toward the window. Without light it would die. But we human beings can do strange things to ourselves. We can be hunger artists, spiritually speaking, and not even die. We can lock ourselves up in the dark for a very long time and even call it living. In the deep recesses of Mammoth Cave there are blind fish that for millions of years have had no eyes, having no need of them. But we humans are amphibious creatures. We can choose. We can, if we get lucky, walk out of the cave of self and after a little preliminary dazzlement be at home in an exciting new world. If to be human is to have an affinity with spirit, let us drink.

[2 April 2000]

* * *

When you hear people say "Christ is risen", think of it as an event that happens inside of you. That's the place where it really matters.

[23 April 2000 (Easter)]

* * *

You have to go deep into the darkness to find the light. Wisdom is a hard thing to come by. It is the product of many mistakes.

[11 June 2000]

* * *

The mystic vibrations in the blood and the beatings of that mighty heart have been going on for the past hour without our hardly being aware of them. We acknowledge the great Sustainer of our being.

[18 June 2000]

* * *

The Spirit is more powerful, persistent, and urgent than we usually realise. The force in the seed thirsts for the light and is not satisfied until it comes into it. Conception begins when two pairs of eyes connect and everything else drops away into insignificance.

[24 December 2000]

* * *

To me the Spirit is like juice coming down a stem.

God is like a Möbius strip, an experience of the paradox of infinity within limitations.

[undated; Pendle Hill on the Road]

* * *

Beyond the itches and thirsts of this world, the pains and stings, is a realm of peace and perfect calm. Imagine that you are in a sailing boat on a wide calm sea. The sail billows gently outward and the wind blows so gently that you feel it only as a freshness in your nostrils, and you move forward almost imperceptibly. The winds of God are always blowing. And we raise our sail.

[undated, 2001]

* * *

The God that cares for us is not tame. There is a wildness there; there is a lilt there, that lifts us into the dance.

[March /2001]

* * *

When I was six years old I was taught how to swim at the town pool. The first thing I had to learn was to put my face in the water and not be afraid of it. I had to learn that I could breathe out and the water wouldn't get in, and I could hold my breath and the water wouldn't get in my nose. The second thing I had to learn was to pull my legs up from the bottom and make like a jellyfish, face down, dangling in the water. I had to learn how to let go into the water, to float.

I had to learn to float before I could swim. The same thing applies to letting ourselves go into God. We have to learn to float before we can swim. We have to relax into the Spirit and let it take us. One of the simplest prayers that I ever learned was to repeat many times "Let go, let God", saying "let go" on each exhalation and "let God" on each inhalation. 'Spirit' is a Latin word meaning 'breath'. If we let ourselves go into the natural rhythms of the breath we can float in the Spirit's healing gentleness. [The last sentence is not quite what I said; I forgot it.]

[23 October 2001]

* * *

"Love was the first motion" according to John Woolman. Each one of us was called into being by an act of love. The merging, nay identity of the physical and the spiritual at the first moment of our being is an incontrovertible fact of our personal history. Each of us was nurtured by many acts of self-denial and caring. And each of us was called to this place by the desire to warm our faces and our hands at that holy fire which we share with others.

[17 February 2002]

* * *

To say "The Lord is risen" requires a big leap of faith, a leap all the way from our ordinary selves to the realm of the ideal. To take that leap requires that we strip ourselves down to our essence and recognise the unity between that essence and the essence of all that is.

[31 March 2002 (Easter)]

* * *

Jacob's ladder is a metaphor for the closeness of earth and heaven. Jacob's ladder is really inside us, even as heaven is inside us. What God is is the offer, always, to be there.

[4 August 2002]

In this advent season we wait for the improbable birth, the impossible dream. Each birth is a mystery, a coming of the eternal into time. Some poets tell us of the mythic, circular, pattern of history. T. S. Eliot says that the beginning and the end are one. When I began this meditation a few minutes ago, I was thinking of the end of the story, the mysterious end, in which quite ordinary people were somehow transformed into the living Christ. The gospels record two instances of this. In the first, Mary thinks she is seeing the gardener outside the tomb, then suddenly she feels or sees that it is Jesus. The second occurs on the way to Emmaus when two disciples encounter a stranger, then sit down with him for a meal. In the breaking of the bread, a symbolic moment in their memory, they feel or see that the stranger is the living Christ. Quakers should understand such transformations. Walt Whitman, who came from a Quaker family, spoke of them often. In his longest and best poem, he imagined in one short passage that in his spiritual self he was undergoing the crucifixion. Then he imagines that he is undergoing the resurrection: he writes "I troop forth replenished with supreme power, one of an average unending procession." The miracle, the improbable birth, the impossible dream, is there for all of us. The average unending procession is all who ever were, all who ever will be, all who are – illumined, seen in the light of the Holy Spirit.

[1 December 2002]

*   *   *

It takes a lot of tears to water the seed.

[11 January 2003]

*   *   *

Napoleon, who was very pragmatic, free-thinking, and not pious, was once discussing religion with his officers, a group of materialists. He swept his hand toward the stars and said "You may talk as long as you please, gentlemen, but who made all that?" I grope toward the edge of the unimaginable expanse of time, billions and billions of years since the universe began. Billions and billions of stars blazed away, living their life, and many of them burning out. Who knows how many billions of planets there are up there around those stars and how many civilisations on them have come and gone. A thousand years is a long time to us, but it is a thousand of those thousand years, maybe more, before we come to the dawn of human history. A seventeenth-century poet, George Herbert I think, wrote what was commonly thought, that all this was created for human convenience, for us. "The stars have us to bed," he wrote; "night draws the curtain, which the sun withdraws." The orthodoxy was, and is, that we are the purpose toward which the whole creation moves. For hundreds of millions of years strange creatures lived and died, their only remains oil deposits under the desert sands. And all this so that we could zip around in our automobiles for a century or so. It stands as a joke on our human pride. The Psalmist said "When I consider the heavens, the work of thy fingers, the moon and the stars which thou hast ordained, what is man that thou art mindful of him?" And yet, "thou hast made him a little lower than the angels, and hast crowned him with glory and honor." We are left staring, our mouths gaping open. We are warmed by that inward stellar explosion with which the universe began.

[2 February 2003]

* * *

Religion might be defined as wanting to do what one ought to do. You might think that that's a definition of morality, but morality is not wanting to do the right thing but doing it anyway, out of a sense of duty. Religion as I have defined it need not necessarily be accompanied by a set of beliefs, in my opinion. It may be a product of grace, which is a gift from God of what one did not necessarily ask for or deserve. But asking helps. Jesus said "ask and you shall receive, seek and you shall find, knock and it will be opened unto you." It is an intricate thing, the relationship between the emotional

and the intellectual in our asking, in our attempts to want to do
what we ought to do. Prayer may not be enough. I remember seeing
on television an interview with a woman who was a drug counsellor.
She had been a crack queen, but then was converted to religion
and was now trying, rather successfully, to help others kick their
addictions. Her religion was of the conservative, evangelical variety.
She was black and knew all about emotionalism in religion. But she
said that in struggling against drug addition prayer was not enough.
"You've got to have a made-up mind," she said. "Prayer won't do you
a bit of good if you don't have a made-up mind." A made-up mind is
a first requirement if we are going to go on from there and want to
do what we ought to do.

[29 June 2003]

* * *

What does not grow will die.
What is not nurtured will not grow.
What is not loved will not be nurtured.
That is why John Woolman said "Love was the first motion."

[14 September 2003]

* * *

Among the sayings of Jesus, one of the wisest and certainly the
wittiest is this: "Sufficient unto the day is the evil thereof." If
we can't escape from old animosities and old guilts, we become
spiritual cripples. And if we are anxious about the future, we miss
the glory in the present.

[29 September 2003]

* * *

There is a moment when the pod opens to deliver its seed, when
the fruit matures on the branch just before falling, when the mind
delivers its thought or warms to a moment of wonder. Capture it,
cherish it, let it nourish you, and absorb the glow.

[18 April 2004]

It can be a long and far journey to reach the centre of our selves. Or it can be in a flash, in a moment of time. At the centre it is remarkably quiet. We are not tossed on the waves of what we desired to possess. The noise is silenced. And yet we can hear the merest whisper of what needs us.

[21 June 2004]

* * *

God, give us courage to face what we would rather turn away from, patience to accept what we cannot avoid, will to work for what we can do, and grace to do all these things without anxiety.

[22 August 2004]

* * *

Be glad for your doubts, for they are a sign that you are alive and real. But work to rise above them. I do not think you will resolve them by intellectual activity, which will probably fail you. I think you will go beyond them only by daring to do what is uncomfortable and then finding that the Spirit will lift you over the gap.

[5 September 2004]

* * *

Every morning we wake up, hoping for the buoyancy that rises above lethargy and defeatism. And we know whence it cometh.

[31 October 2004]

* * *

There is no physical form or symbol that can proclaim all that we are and believe.

There is no form of words that can express all that we feel. That is why we have no creed.

We do not place limits on the divine potential, which expands and bursts all boundaries. [After a discussion in Peace and Service committee about installing a Peace Pole in our yard.]

[14 November 2004]

* * *

There is a reason why revelation must be continuing. The breath
I took five minutes ago built bone and flesh and gave me structure.
But it will not keep me alive now.

[5 December 2004]

* * *

The good that was in you and is in you was infused into your body
at the moment of its conception. It stems from a love that stretches
back aeons of time and that was transmitted forward into you.

[16 January 2005]

* * *

"God's grace is always there" said Enoch. But my light bulb is often
burnt out. Or I neglect to turn on the switch. Or I have one of those
dimmers that makes my light go up and down. Yesterday the light
at the rear door outside the meeting house was missing. So Rich
reached up and screwed in a new bulb. Being in the Spirit takes effort,
conscious intention, or recollection of times when we were connected.

[13 March 2005]

* * *

With so much hatred in the world we wonder what our little
candle can do against the darkness. And then the wind blows and
our candle flickers and goes out. I experienced this literally last
Wednesday. At the vigil on Raymond Avenue my candle flickered
in the wind and then went out. But I turned to the person next
to me and got a light. We need each other. We need the Afghan
quilt thrown across the lap of life. [Diane-Ellen had spoken of the
90-year-old woman who offered her Afghan quilt she had made,

but Diane-Ellen said no, she would need it herself. Then later she saw the quilt spread across the lap of a man amputated at the knees for diabetes. The woman had given it to him. All the people in the group were gathered around, and the old man's eyes were so happy.]

[11 September 2005]

* * *

Finding God is a contact sport. Jacob had to wrestle with the angel to be saved from himself. Wrestling makes us sweat. A minister in Connecticut back in the seventeenth century said, famously, "You must take up your cross, and it will make you sweat." Yesterday, in our dining room, the Financial Services Committee of New York Yearly Meeting wrestled with columns of figures that did not conveniently match with each other. Then as I looked out the window I saw Fred Doneit gathering up fallen branches and dirt from our parking lot, putting them in a wheelbarrow and taking them to the woodlot. He was sweating. There seems to be a force in the world that litters our lawns and our lives with things we do not want. I remember how Grete Carpenter kept reminding us of the reality of evil in the world, and I remember the way each time we pinned evil to the mat with our convenient formulas. But it kept getting up. Every week here in meeting I wrestle with the two faces of God, the benign and the fearsome. It takes a lot of faith to get beyond our doubts. And where – whence – does it come from? I come up against the blank wall of that question, which I did not anticipate when I started talking. The only answer I have is the trembling that I feel right now at this moment.

[18 September 2005]

* * *

The rains came and the wind blew and the house that was built on sandy foundations was washed away. Much of the modern civilisation of which we are so proud is built on sandy foundations, on selfishness and the arrogance of power. It is fragile, and the towers of Babel and of Manhattan were toppled with a push. The house that endures is built on rock. The Rock of Ages that millions of people's testimony in their hearts has given voice to.

[9 October 2005]

* * *

Shoes are a powerful memorial symbol. When a person dies we sometimes say "Those shoes will be hard to fill." When my brother's best friend died, he inherited a pair of his shoes, and he sometimes wore them. When my brother died 44 years ago, I inherited that pair of shoes. They were too big for me, but I kept them for a while. There is a saying that before criticising someone we should walk two miles in his shoes. Last Wednesday in Vassar Chapel I shook the hand of a man who had just decorated the boots representing his son's death. "Did you know John?" he said. I said "No, but I was just looking at his picture attached to the boots." In grief all the world is one.

[20 November 2005]

* * *

William Wordsworth began a poem with these words:

The world is too much with us; late and soon,
Getting and spending, we lay waste our powers;
Little we see in Nature that is ours;
We have given our hearts away...

I have spent my life getting and spending, often for things I did not need. For example, when I was in college I bought tons of books at second-hand bookstores. Many of them I have never read. I said I was saving them for my retirement; some of them I have now read, others I will never get to. And this is just one category. Enoch spoke of losing his watch. When I was in prison I gave away my watch, because one of my fellow inmates asked for it. I expected to get it

59

back, but I never did. We got separated, sent to different jails, and I never saw him again. When I was in prison I went through a whole process of divestiture. My clothes and my wallet were taken away from me temporarily. I felt a kind of purity, which I have never quite recovered. Late and soon, getting and spending, I have laid waste my powers.

[8 January 2006]

* * *

Deep into the dark, hidden in the ground, the seed stirs and flexes. The spring warmth reaches it, the rains unclench it. Even so, sometimes we need to go deep into the dark to see the light.

[22 January 2006]

* * *

[Olivia, age six, was swinging her legs.]
Everybody likes to swing. If your feet can't touch the floor, there's nothing for your legs to do but swing. When I was growing up, a favourite kind of music was called swing. It was very fast and was a lot of fun. On the playground, everybody likes to swing. You swing up, and then you swing back, and then you pull up again and again, higher and higher, as far as you can get. You're really flying, but the seat under you is firm, held by the chains, and it holds you, and you feel safe. And the earth swings around the sun. It's moving all the time, fast, and yet it's held firmly, as if it were on the end of a long chain, and it doesn't go flying off into space. And you're safe. God is like that, always moving, and yet a firm ground underneath you.

[26 February 2006]

* * *

Jesus said "Take no thought for tomorrow, for tomorrow will take care of itself." Usually, this is interpreted literally, as if tomorrow were April 28, 2006. But I think tomorrow also includes after we are dead. I don't think death is anything to be afraid of. We can approach it with confidence and take no thought of what will happen to us afterwards. A great deal of religion has been based on fear, particularly on fear of death. Whole millennia have been devoted to this fear of death. People have been inculcated with the idea of "the fear of God". I don't think God is there to be feared. We can live, live with the confidence that we are accepted, that we don't have to earn our way into God's favour, as if God were a king to graciously reward his favourites. God is the very ground of our being, the substance and essence of all that we are. We do not have to wait for our acceptance. We are already and always there.

[27 April 2006]

* * *

Viola and I went to the opera yesterday and saw *Lohengrin*. The first part of the overture was mysterious and thrilling, almost an analogue of a spiritual experience. It started with a pianissimo so faint that you weren't sure you were hearing the few violins that were playing, then it slowly grew as more violins were added and twined into a complex harmony, a shimmer, an icy breath, something electric.

People come to our meeting for the first time, hoping to find something that speaks to them out of the silence. Often they go away, disappointed, not having heard it. Sometimes they see a faint glimmer at the edge of the dawn, a pianissimo shimmer, and they come back, hungry. The hunger, which is ourselves, feeds on a mystery. The mystery calls forth ourselves, new, into the dawn.

[30 April 2006]

* * *

People come to us from time to time looking for God. And we tell them, The Divine is already inside of you; you just have to let it out. But that is a very tangled ball of string. And we know the story. We look for the end and wrestle with it and after a while maybe we've made a little progress. Then a voice calls to us "My Child! I am yours."

[14 May 2006]

That power manifests itself as a supreme stillness that draws us to
the centre, where we feel the engendering force that makes the grass
grow and the birds sing.

[3 September 2006]

*   *   *

Every cell in our body knows what it has to do.
We don't have to tell it, and sometimes we can't even control it.
The skin knows to grow over the wound,
The heart to beat,
The eyelid to blink.

[31 December 2006]

*   *   *

In meeting for worship it is usually my experience that I have to
go through the darkness to get to the light. This is true first on
a literal level. After the whirl of thoughts calms down, my mind
drifts toward not thinking at all, toward darkness. Sometimes, for
a split second, it's like going to sleep, like going through a black
hole in my mind and going through into something that looks a
little like dawn. This is true on a symbolic level too. I used to think
of myself as a pretty optimistic person. I remember that at my
mother's 100th birthday party in 1999 I made a little speech about
how my mother had lived through the rise and fall of fascism,
Nazism, and communism. And in 1999 it looked as if the problem
of federal budget deficits was behind us and we were entering into
a wonderful new age. But I don't have that easy optimism anymore
about what's happening in the world. We slide deeper and deeper
into the quicksand of the Middle East, with no solution in sight.
We see foolishness in high places. The atmosphere is warming up
inexorably and is very close to that tipping point where all that ice
melts and the water pours down over Holland and Bangladesh,
Calcutta, Shanghai, and even Lower Manhattan. In the world, as
I look around, I find an inexorable darkness closing down. But

the world is not the end of it. For thousands of years we've been hearing "In the world you have tribulation, but be of good cheer, for I have overcome the world." The world is not our final resting place, though it is the only home we know. There is an Inside to all that Outside. And the Inside is filled with light.

[14 January 2007]

* * *

Every spring all nature presses forward urging to break into blossom.

[16 September 2007]

* * *

I need a reference note to tune my mind to. In an orchestra the reference note is A, 440 cycles per second. The oboe sounds A, and all the other instruments tune to match it and then tune the other strings in relation to it. We have a piano tuner here in the room with us, and I think of the last time I heard a piano tuned. Each note has three strings that have to be adjusted to match each other. As they are tightened the note is repeatedly struck; it is jangling and slightly irritating until finally the right note pops into place and the sound is beautiful and we say "ah". Everyone knows the difference between noise and music. Noise is random, with sounds clashing against each other, scratchy and irritating. Music is organised, harmonious, going somewhere, invigorating, calming, soothing, healing. We shun noise and seek out music, sometimes paying a lot of money for it. We are hungry for harmony. Most of the time the mind is full of noise, randomness, jumble, like someone surfing rapidly through a hundred television channels. But sometimes, looking deeply in the silence, I can almost see as a physical presence the Inward Light that we talk about. Listening in the silence we will hopefully find the reference note to tune our minds to.

[30 September 2007]

* * *

Beauty is always there for us whenever our glance gathers it and we gaze deeply into the colours, dimensions, shape, and coherence of what is there, penetrating through the surface into the deep heart that is beating beneath it and supporting it.

[4 November 2007]

* * *

We spend part of our day criticising others. And we spend part of our day criticising ourselves. Between blame and shame we feel no peace. To break out of this we need to focus on the budding goodness that we can find in others and in ourselves. St Paul said "Whatsoever things are good, whatsoever things are true, whatsoever things are honest, whatsoever things are of good report, think on these things." What we dwell upon, that we will become.

[20 January 2008]

* * *

Some of the most precious things in life are very simple. The air we breathe. The light we see by. The warmth that surrounds us. But that warmth is also inside of us, carried by every living being. It needs to be fed. I think of building a fire. It begins with something very small, a spark. It needs to be fed. We nurture it, and it grows. It also has to be moderated, kept under control. The fire warms us. We bask in that glory.

[5 October 2008]

* * *

"Peace I leave with you, my peace I give unto you: not as the world giveth, give I unto you." These words of Jesus speak of what rises above the tensions and torment, what rises and floats in the kind eyes of Him who loved us before we ever were.

[21 December 2008]

* * *

When Jesus spoke of giving He spoke of two kinds. The world's gifts are external. They have a shape, a size, a price, a place. The gifts given by Jesus are all priceless, internal. Joy, love, hope, calmness, steadiness. The gift of self-assurance makes it possible to absorb enmity and injury without the need to retaliate. It is possible to do this only because we are connected to the Source of power that is at the centre of the universe.

[24 December 2008]

* * *

I don't think the peace testimony is a statement, not even so powerful a statement as the declaration of 1660 or the words of Jesus in the Sermon on the Mount, precious as they are in guiding and inspiring us. The peace testimony is not words. It is not something abstract. It is our actions. It is not even our inactions, our passivity, something that we don't do. It is something positive, the things that we do do. It is not even something done by a group. The peace testimony has to be an expression of feeling in an individual, the actions that arise from a person responding to the Inward Light.

I think we make a mistake in saying that the peace testimony is an absolute and requires that we opt for perfect purity. Integrity does not mean that we are perfectly pure. I know that I am not. I make compromises every day, and I am making compromises right now in being here in this comfortable place. Everything we do is an approximation of the ideal and is full of compromises.

[25 January 2009]

* * *

What is the sound of one hand clapping?
Now you know.
It fills all time and space.

[8 February 2009]

* * *

There is a powerful urge in the world to create things that are beautiful. But beautiful things are often very fragile. I am thinking of a butterfly's wings and its beautiful colours. This week I saw some photographs of tropical butterflies with transparent wings, clear windows splashed with colour. Incredibly beautiful. But butterflies don't live very long. Or I am thinking of the bowl of daffodils we have at home. They started opening on Wednesday, and today they are already beginning to shrivel. Human beings try to create beautiful things, and ones that are more permanent. Words can last a long time. Everywhere and always human beings have been multiplying words, on papyrus, on clay, on paper, reaching for an imperishable beauty. Or they work in stone and make sculptures or cathedrals. I remember a room in Florence, Italy. In the centre is Michelangelo's monumental masterpiece, the statue of David, twenty or so feet high, polished and perfect. But the statues that spoke to me even more were the ones in another room that Michelangelo left unfinished at the end of his life. They are rough, rugged, and powerful. To the very end he kept chipping away, getting his many urgent ideas roughed out, and didn't have time to finish and polish. What is that something in us? Without much expectation of creating anything really significant, we ordinary people keep chipping away. There is a something in us, an urge toward the imperishable.

[22 March 2009]

* * *

I have been to several meetings of the kind where people say "Praise the Lord" a number of times. And so I have thought about what it means to praise God. The problem is that there is a long tradition of praising God and hating the world, of praising God and hating sinners, of praising God and hating one's 'enemies', of praising God and killing those enemies. But I don't look upon God and the world as opposed to each other. I think God is expressed through the world, through the physical. That's where love comes in; God loves through us. The earth is beautiful, not ugly. And so, at Easter, we recognise that the earth has been given back to us.

[Easter, 2009]

* * *

The prayer of St Francis begins "Lord, make me an instrument of Thy peace. Where there is hatred, let me sow love." If I hear that with the word spelled s-e-w, I imagine someone embroidering the word 'love' with gorgeous colored threads. The result is beautiful, a work of art, to be displayed on a wall and admired. But still, "love" is only a symbol, a word. But if 'sow' is heard rightly, I visualise someone scattering or planting seeds. It takes a long time for a plant to produce seeds. Seed production is the goal toward which its whole growth is directed and in which it culminates. The seed is the fulfilment and also the beginning of life. But love is costly. Love is risky. And so – do we hold ourselves back?

[8 November 2009]

* * *

To be inspired is to breathe in. Spirit is breath. But we can't breathe in unless we also breathe out, give back. We live in a rhythmic economy, decreed from the beginning, not to be escaped.

[21 March 2010]

* * *

They tried to kill it, but it escaped. And it blossomed. They kept on trying to kill it, over and over again. But it escaped. And it blossomed.

[4 April 2010, (Easter)]

* * *

[Eddie, an inmate attender at the Green Haven prison Quaker worship group, had just died. He had a few months earlier sent to our meeting a collection of colourful paper flowers.]

I have seen many flowers in bowls. They all grew pale, they withered, and were thrown out. Right now I am looking at the bowl of Eddie's paper flowers on the piano. They will not grow pale, they will not wither, they will not get thrown out. What's remarkable about these flowers is not just that they are beautiful, it is that they were made with very limited resources: what Eddie had available to him in the prison. They are made of toilet tissue, Kool Aid colouring, and Eddie's genius. Eddie made full use of what he had.

On our dining table at home we have a hot pad, also made of paper. Sheets of old magazine paper were rolled up tightly and coiled into little squares, which were fastened together into a complex colourful hot pad. The person who made it, in Latin America, obviously didn't get paid very much for all that careful, skillful labour. That person made full use of limited resources.

Last Friday when the meeting women's group, the Crones, met in our apartment, I went downstairs to the VCR in the lounge and watched a film that I had taped off the air ten years earlier but had never looked at. It was based on Thomas Hardy's *The Mayor of Casterbridge*, a novel that I had never read. Then, yesterday, I read the last fifty pages of the novel. On the next-to-last page I found a statement about how people with limited resources can find satisfaction in life, by making full use of what they have. Hardy speaks of microscopic enlargement of "those minute forms of satisfaction that offer themselves to everybody not in positive pain." In other words, focus on the things that everybody has. The air we breathe. The colour green in the grass. The aroma of food. The solidity of the ground on which we stand. The richness of the Spirit that cradles us.

[20 June 2010]

* * *

Comfort is what we try for. But growth doesn't come from comfort; it comes from challenge. Without challenge we grow humdrum and fade. What does not grow will gradually die or ossify and become a relic. Quakerism is a religion not of conventionalism and comfort, not of dogmas and rules, not of holding on. It is a religion of abundance. It spills over any rigid cup that seeks to contain it. To be a Quaker is to be not afraid of the unknown. It is to launch out in it, to be a seeker.

[8 August 2010]

* * *

Conflict is not always bad. It can be the very condition of transformation. A physical analogy can be drawn. Some chemical reactions require high heat. Conflict raises our inner temperature. Saul was struck down on the road to Damascus by the inner conflict raging within him because he was persecuting the Christians. He became a new man, Paul, the leader of the Christians. Some years ago I read a book, called *Release*, by a man who went by the name of Starr Dailey. He was a prisoner, so recalcitrant that they couldn't do anything with him, so they stuck him in the hole, solitary confinement. There he wrestled with his inner demons and something inside him welled up and he became a changed man. He was released from prison, both the outer and the inner prisons, and he went on to become a noted Christian evangelist. And an evangelist knows that it is sometimes the person who is fighting him the hardest who is on the verge of giving in and being released, becoming a changed person. Under tension and heat, the Light Within can break out and drive us to our knees.

[12 September 2010]

* * *

If we say "God loves us" I think that means "God loves through us." But love must have objects. It must do something. Love creates families, cathedrals, paintings, poems. If you have fallen in love, and I think you have, you remember that it was like a shaft of sunlight breaking through clouds. A golden glow spread everywhere around you and in you. And everything else fell away into the background.

[16 October 2010]

This is a time for getting down to bedrock, away from the frippery and falsity, the consumerism and sentimentality. We want what is real. This applies to the gospels too. At the centre of the Christmas story there is one fact that is bedrock, too real to have been invented. Jesus was born in a stable. Not in a palace, as the makers of pretty fables would have had it. And towards the end of Jesus's life there is one thing he said that reaches out and grabs me. It is real. Jesus said "I was an hungered and you fed me; I was thirsty and you gave me drink; I was a stranger and you took me in; naked, and you clothed me; I was sick and you visited me; I was in prison and you came unto me." But when did we do all this? they asked. And the answer came back, authoritative and final: "Inasmuch as you have done it unto one of the least of these my brethren, you have done it unto me." This is the Resurrection. Jesus is there, in everyone. If you miss this, you have missed him entirely.

[24 December 2010]

* * *

I am struck by the contrast between surface water and the water deep down in the earth. On the surface the water mixes with dirt and we have mud. In the winter, snow banks along the streets are blackened with automobile exhaust and melt in salty rivulets.

I used to live on the side of a mountain in New Paltz and our water came from a well. The road in winter was a mucky mess. But the water filtered down through 90 feet of dirt and leaves and rock, and when it came up from our well it was clear and sparkling and delicious.

I think of our world, in which we are enmeshed in surfaces, dismayed by the muck and disorder, political conflict, intractable problems, and wars – evil that seems to engulf everything.

I remember my last visit to Ruth Lewis Hall, a Friend in her 70s in New Paltz. She was dying of cancer, and this was was just three days before she died. She walked out of her bedroom to greet me. She was terribly emaciated and scarcely looked like herself. But she never said a word about the pain she was feeling. Her eyes were bright and sparkled with an intensity that I had never seen in her before. Her smile had an incredible radiance, unworldly. She was tapping something deep down, under the surface.

We come into this quiet place on Sunday morning to worship. We tap into the water that runs deep. A spirit that we call divine says, encouragingly, Outside it's all mud and slush, but I am more than all that.

[23 January 2011]

*   *   *

The arising of consciousness in the world's history came out of nowhere. It was a dramatic break with the billions of years of machine-driven evolving that had gone on before.

Perhaps last week you watched on *Jeopardy!* as Watson, an IBM computer, easily vanquished the best human contestants that could be arrayed against him. Then yesterday I read in *Time* magazine an interview with the IBM scientist chiefly responsible for creating Watson. Does Watson approach the level of a precocious child? No, Watson doesn't feel or understand anything. Does Watson have any plans for the future? No, Watson doesn't plan; he just does what he was programmed to do, which is play *Jeopardy!*. Watson has no consciousness. He can't do what the simplest child does easily: cry when he feels bad, smile when he feels good. What a mystery we are! How glorious!

[27 February 2011]